D1080997

THIS IS A CARLTON BOOK

The Dog Logo and Photographs ©
2007 Artlist INTERNATIONAL Inc
Text and Design copyright © 2007
Carlton Books Limited

This edition published in 2007 by
Carlton Books Ltd
20 Mortimer Street
London
W1T 3JW

A CIP catalogue for this book is available
from the British Library.

ISBN 978 1 84442 190 9

Publishing Manager: Penny Craig
Art Director: Clare Baggaley
Design: Vicky Rankin
Production: Lisa Moore

Printed and bound in Singapore

THE DOG

Artlist Collection

FUN **PUPPIES**

CARLTON

Miniature Schnauzer

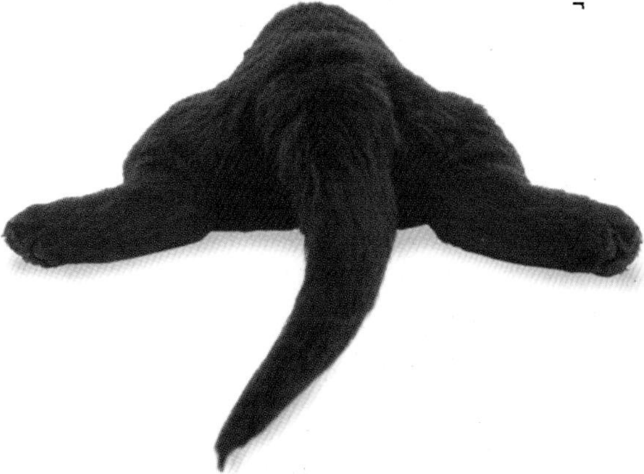

Flat-Coated Retriever

Flat-Coated Retriever

Shetland Sheepdog

Miniature Dachshund

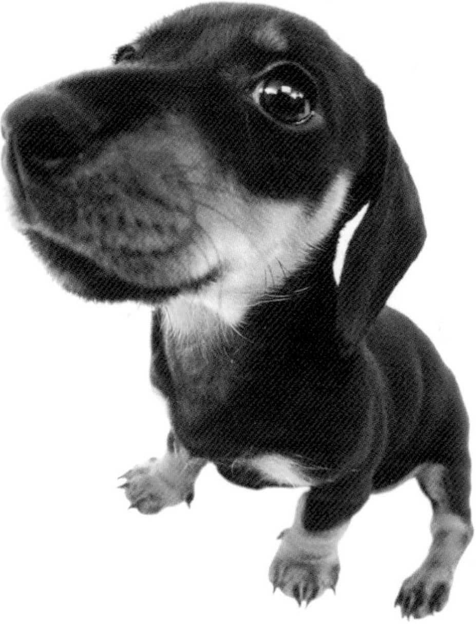

Miniature Dachshund

Beagle

Yorkshire Terrier

Polish Lowland Sheepdog

Dalmatian

Bernese Mountain Dog

Poodle

Pug

Siberian Husky

Maltese

Pembroke Welsh Corgi

Pembroke Welsh Corgi

French Bulldog

Schnauzer

Bull Terrier

Cavalier King Charles Spaniel

Cavalier King Charles Spaniel

Newfoundland

Papillon

Chihuahua

Miniature Pinscher

Miniature Pinscher

Boxer

Bichon Frise

Tibetan Spaniel

Tibetan Spaniel

West Highland White Terrier

Afghan Hound

Old English Sheepdog

Irish Setter

Saluki

Japanese Spitz

German Shepherd

Shih-Tzu

Shih-Tzu